TOWN AND COUNTRY PUBLIC LIBRARY DISTRICT

3 2990 00096 7665

WITHDRAWN

W9-BPS-840

TOWN & COUNTRY
PUBLIC LIBRARY DISTRICT
320 E. NORTH ST.
ELBURN, IL 60119

Table of Contents

Machines on the Farm

Grab your keys.

Get ready to work!

Farmers use machines to

make jobs faster and easier.

Tractors

Check out the hardest workers on the farm. Tractors pull, lift, plow, and plant.

Climb into the cab!

Most tractor cabs are

air-conditioned. Some cabs

even have computers

and GPS devices.

Machines for Growing Crops

Tractors pull plows.

Plows get fields ready

for planting. A plow's blades

lift, flip, and loosen soil.

A seed drill pokes holes in the soil. Then the drill drops seeds into the holes and covers up the seeds.

Weeds steal food and water

from crops. Row cultivators

keep fields free from weeds.

Metal discs dig up the weeds.

Machines for Harvesting Crops

Combines harvest, or gather, grains. Rolling spikes feed grain into the combine. Then grain is removed from the husks and cleaned.

Cotton harvesters pick

fluffy white cotton.

These machines move by

themselves. They can pick

six rows of cotton at once.

Balers roll up grass
and silage. Bales can
weigh more than 1 ton
(0.9 metric tons). The bales
feed animals during winter.

Town & Country
Public Library District
320 E. North St.
Elburn, IL 60119

Glossary

bale—a large bundle of grass, silage, straw, or hay tied tightly together

blade—the cutting part of a tool

crop—a plant farmers grow in large amounts, usually for food; farmers grow crops such as corn, soybeans, and grains

cultivator—a machine that prepares land for crops

disc—a flat, thin, round object

drill—a machine that makes holes

GPS—an electronic tool that uses satellites to find the location of objects; GPS stands for global positioning system

grain—the seed of a cereal plant such as wheat, rice, corn, rye, or barley

harvest—to gather crops that are ripe

husk—the dry covering of a grain

machine—a piece of equipment that is used to do a job

silage—grass or other plants that are made into animal food

spike—a sharp, pointy object

Read More

Coppendale, Jean. *Tractors and Farm Vehicles.* Mighty Machines. Richmond Hill, Ont.: Firefly Books, 2010.

Dayton, Connor. *Tractors.* Farm Machines. New York: PowerKids Press, 2012.

Dickmann, Nancy. *Farm Machines.* World of Farming. Chicago: Heinemann Library, 2011.

Internet Sites

FactHound offers a safe, fun way to find Internet sites related to this book. All of the sites on FactHound have been researched by our staff.

Here's all you do:

Visit *www.facthound.com*

Type in this code: 9781491421185

 Check out projects, games and lots more at **www.capstonekids.com**

Critical Thinking Using the Common Core

1. Why do farmers use balers? (Key Ideas and Details)

2. Look at the pictures. Why do you think a tractor's wheels are so big? (Integration of Knowledge and Ideas)

Index

Word Count: 168
Grade: 1
Early-Intervention Level: 21